About the Author

Tahlia Gobius drinks French Earl Grey and Melbourne Breakfast Tea. She was born in Australia but is a third-culture Kid. Tahlia plays the piano. She has two dogs, their names are Mele and Bella. Her sweet spot is driving around listening to music. She would be nowhere without the support of her family. In the mornings, Tahlia sits out in the sun and writes poetry; now, she supposes, the poems have found their way to you.

Becoming

Tahlia Gobius

Becoming

Olympia Publishers
London

www.olympiapublishers.com
OLYMPIA PAPERBACK EDITION

Copyright © Tahlia Gobius 2024

The right of Tahlia Gobius to be identified as author of this work has been asserted in accordance with sections 77 and 78 of the Copyright, Designs and Patents Act 1988.

All Rights Reserved

No reproduction, copy or transmission of this publication may be made without written permission.
No paragraph of this publication may be reproduced, copied or transmitted save with the written permission of the publisher, or in accordance with the provisions of the Copyright Act 1956 (as amended).

Any person who commits any unauthorised act in relation to this publication may be liable to criminal prosecution and civil claims for damage.

A CIP catalogue record for this title is available from the British Library.

ISBN: 978-1-83543-018-7

First Published in 2024

Olympia Publishers
Tallis House
2 Tallis Street
London
EC4Y 0AB

Printed in Great Britain

Dedication

I dedicate this book to my family: Mum, Dad, Lani, Danya and Tatiana. Without your patience, comfort and encouragement, I never would have made it past the toughest times and lived to write about it.

Note from the Author

'becoming' is a collection of poems I have written about my own experiences.

Some of the poems were written in the moment, some have been penned in retrospect.

Some of the emotions experienced were transient, others are reoccurring.

There are five categories of poems;
drowning,
surviving,
coping,
healing and
blossoming.

Please be forewarned, many of the poems focus on themes of mental illness and suicide.

drowning

part one

Though my body is intact,
most of the scars are beneath the surface.

There are burns on my liver,
from handling and filtering out the pain.

My heart bears stretch marks
from accommodating those I love,
along with my own desires.

My lungs are discoloured
from breathing in and out all the negativity.

There is shrinkage in my brain,
as it shies away from reality.

The eyes, however,
are a window to the inner suffering.
Come closer and see my story,
embedded deep inside my irises.

I fell off a waterfall
And all things considered
I was glad
It had finally come to pass
I lifted my head for a moment's reprieve
And saw two paths ahead
One was long and windy; treacherous rapids
The other, all I could see was the sky.

Goodbye
Can't say when I fell in, or
Where I come from
'Cause everything is rushing
By so fast I don't recognise a thing

People running alongside
Shouting advice I can't hear
They quickly disappear
bubble bubble, gush rush
constant tempo, march of time

clothes billow
tangle tighter
lead shoes, but they won't let you touch the bottom
preserved by an instinct of
frantic kicking,
gasping for breath

freezing water in my eyes,
up my nose
gushing down my throat
it's punching me, swirling me
churning me, flipping me

so, when I see the end hurrying towards me,
you will excuse my choice to go limp
to let myself be taken by the current
and maybe hope I'll end up in the sky
you can't blame me; if I'd tried, it might not have saved me.

What if what is to come is not worth it?

What if it doesn't equate with all the hurt and pain of before?

I wish I could be saying that everything made me stronger, and I can handle tomorrow.

But I can't.

I'm not proud of who I am. I don't believe that I've ended up a better person.

All I can see are the deficits, how I don't live up to the person I used to be.

The best is not yet to come if all I need is to end now.

There is no peace.

I don't have the strength to handle more change, and I can't live with life as it is.

You feel like you have been punctured,
and all of your energy rushed out,
leaving you deflated.
Every step is heavy.

In each movement you make,
Your body feels disconnected from your brain.
Your mind is detached;
estranged from reality.

You are despondent,
fading into the gloom.

Everywhere you see a shadow,
but if you wade through the anguish of the mind,
one thought is illuminated.

The singular goal that makes all the effort
of the day manageable:

The End

I am bitter.
I am judgemental.
I'm impatient, unhelpful and hurting.

I'm a prisoner of life
A life I don't want to live.
I am a prisoner of love
I love and it kills me.

I don't yearn for the future.
I don't have dreams, aspirations.
Except… for it all to end.
So just let me be.

I'm breaking with pain.
I can feel the cracks deepening along my body;
Shattering
I can barely breathe with wanting
Begging, pleading, hoping, screaming
To tumble into a cold unknowing.
Abandon waiting, wishing, wanting
for nothing.

Toes tap; distraction
fists form; protection
thoughts chug along.

Click clack, faster now
then faster, with reckless abandon
violent rocking; calm me.

The vice slowly tightens,
suffocating.
agony runs deeper; unfathomable
tears roll; give up
Building up to detonation.

Past the point of help
Done with holding on
Slipping; I've tried my best
Now award me with peace.

I see the bright colours, smell the perfumes of the garden…
But I am a dull grey.

The children run around, shrieking and laughing…
But my limbs have stiffened.

Music with a strong beat plays, and people dance…
But I cannot be heard.

Beach-goers swim and tan in the summer sun…
But I am as cold as ice.

It may look like I am still here…
But I am already gone.

Everything is pitch black,
Nothing matters any more,
I want, I need it to end.

I am apart from the world,
In a place no one can understand,
So little is tying me here.

I take a deep breath,
Thoughts racing,
Pulled towards the obvious choice.

I take a step…
And choose life.

It takes more courage
to live than to die.

surviving

part two

It's not the light you expected.
It's the ethereal glaze left on the waves closest to shore,
after the dregs of sunlight have drained.

For a moment, it is neither dark,
nor light, but your eyes adjust.

When the glare of day is too much,
and the depth of night consumes you,
you brave a step into the in between.
It's a tentative grasp for hope.

I am a bear
in a cave.
I eat,
I sleep.
I am safe
under the cover
of darkness.

My senses
are dulled.
The worries
of the world
can wait.

I grunt
and groan.
I await
the spring.

—hibernating.

> "We had nowhere else to go,
> no choice but to go on living."
> –Meiko Kawakami

There is no other planet to choose from,
No button to respawn as another human,
No option to radically change this life.

I am not distraught because I must die,
but because 'there is no other choice
but to go on living'.

Now I must adjust my mindset,
and get down to the nitty-gritty
of life.

Just barely made it through the night
Awoke with some fire
till I quickly started flickering.

Just barely stayed awake on the drive home
Eyelids fluttering, stumbling back to bed
Caterpillar to butterfly and reset in record time.

Enough spirit to function but not thrive
Enough joy to notice the sting when it's crushed
Never knowing what the next moment holds.

I have an empty space,
deeper than the chasm my ribcage contains.

I march on, faulting and failing, growing and learning.

I take my penance, but how can I thrust it upon another?
Just barely awake enough to engage,
broken enough to emanate pain.

Vulnerable, drained; is this what I have to dispense?
A half-life, a cursed life, a fucked-up mess.

Just barely making it through the day;
Just barely alive.

Anxiety stirs in my chest.
Climb inside my body and
experience it with me.

My heart squeezes and expands,
at the same time,
throughout its cavity.

I push on the back of my
clenched teeth with my
tongue, my breathing
is shallow.

Every breath is heavy,
a sinking feeling
in my diaphragm.

The voices around me get louder,
like they are closing in on me.
The lights are brighter, overwhelming
my eyes.

It feels as if something is pulling
the back of my tongue
into my throat.
I open my mouth to speak
but my brain feels like it is
working overtime,
only a tiny section of it
is co-operating.

I cannot find the right words.
I cannot communicate my frustration,
and the reluctance to take any
action which will further my pain.

I become short. The world is spinning.

Let me off.

So many years of stress,
of being diminished,
have left my grey matter a shadow of its former self.

The heroic hippocampus crumbled,
refusing to store memories the way it once did.

The powerful prefrontal cortex has shrunk,
along with my ability to make sense of the world.

And the once amiable amygdala is swollen and aggressive,
colouring everything that I think.

They've left me with no motivation,
no follow through, and little hope for the future.

Even daring dopamine won't play like it used to.

But I cannot blame my brain,
it has fought a valiant war.
I know, deep down,
that my soldiers continue to march into battle,
to the beat of my heart;
braced to face whatever each day has thrown at them.

Survival is possible if you put your mind to it.

It's raining in my chest cavity again today.
It's mostly a drizzle of discontent.

Lately, we've weathered the storms of agitation,
the lighting strikes of panic,
and the fog of anxiety,
but no clear skies and blue.

The cold permeates into the inner chambers of my heart,
and I haven't much hope for the sun.

When you lose someone who is a part of you,
Where does the rest of your love for them go?

It cascades out in waterfalls of tears.
It bundles into the achy part of your chest.
The love spirals around your painful thoughts.
It shoots out the ends of your fingertips as your hands shake.

You learn that the one that you lost
has given you one last gift.
All the love you held for them,
you can now invest in yourself.

Apply it to your wounds.
Wrap it around your tired body.
Use it to soften your memories.
Keep pushing on.

The moon rays stream through my window
casting the shadow of the bed frame onto the wall
my shadow is there too
I reflect as I stare at the bars of my life.

Time drags on
fast enough to get caught up in the flow
gushing deep into my soul
slow enough to break me

The moon mocks me
a grin
Doesn't it know I don't feel like smiling?
Doesn't it know I feel a kind of pain?

The kind of pain that emanates
from the bottom of my ribcage
that drives slivers underneath my fingernails
the weight of it in my bones.

The moon seems close enough to palm
Sanity seems close enough to gain
Don't you know you tease me?
Don't you know I'm almost there?

coping

part three

I come alive when I give a gift
Especially when I make it myself.

I treasure time with the family
And I find different ways that I can help.

I love it when I am creating art
And soaking in the beauty around me.

Yet, there is something that's holding me back
Something still stops me from being free.

Subliminal sadness, just underneath
Subtly holding me from life; apart.

Unable to focus on the future
Like joy slowly leaking from my heart.

Though I have got coping down to an art
I ask; is it always going to hurt?

I've been awake since the early hours,
going over everything.

My bag is packed with everything I could possible need;
a compass,
a map,
weapons in case of foreign invaders.

I tell myself over and over that it will be worth the energy
I put into it,
even though I know I might be bending the truth.

"Just start, go for it,"
I chant inside my head.
I take a deep breath,
ready to face my destiny.

I lift off one corner of the covers,
sit up,
swivel my legs,
and step out of bed.

"All the women. In me. Are tired,"
Nayyirah Waheed, *Nejma*

>The woman who enjoys her creative side,
>The woman who loves to sleep,
>The woman who gets unreasonably anxious,
>The woman who puts on makeup for fun,
>The woman who gains joy out of giving gifts and
>The woman who can't imagine life without her family...

>All the women in me...
>Have gone on strike.

>The shopfront is boarded up.
>They can't be expected to work
>without being paid enough energy.

>They are tired.

>Call them when something changes.

I chose life.
But I still taste the past.

Reminders come up like acid reflux.
They sting my throat,
leave an off taste in my mouth,
my throat dry.

They say, "No matter how much you
think you've moved on, we will
always be here to remind you of
the way out."

Some days, it is startling,
others I know what to expect.
But it never. leaves. me. alone.

hospital

I put one foot in front of the other
following a steady beat.

I sit, I smile, I add my two cents
But the room sends waves of anxiety into my heart.

I eat, I mingle, I'm grateful
for the food and the company.

I recline and receive
magnetic pulses of hope, right into my brain.

I listen
to sweet words through headphones.

I swallow, I sip, check in
and allow my freedom to be institutionalised.

I paint, I draw,
gaining admiration and companionship.

I lie, eyes closed
done for one day, bracing for another.

The sun is coming out now
here comes the sun.

I am the lone caretaker at the Museum of Me
I had once preserved all the important
exhibits with diligence and ease.

I polished my achievements and
showcased each emotion
for every guest to take in.
Each section was intertwined,
highlighting exactly who I was.

Lately, my museum has fallen into disarray.
Things are fragmented,
hidden behind different layers of dust.
The Hall of Emotions is muted,
except for sporadic eruptions.

There is no coherency from exhibit to exhibit,
and the range of people who walk through the doors
is severely limited.

Things have declined to the point
that I am sincerely looking into employing
new management.

Death came to visit
He stole away in the night
And took you with him
Everything froze
It seemed like the end
But Life was not finished.

If everything is too much,
If you are hurting,
If life is frustrating you,
If you cannot go on…

Sit with me in this space.
You don't have to say a word.

Just be.

healing

part four

gold streams in my window.

It touches the darkest parts of my soul
and fizzles. a shadow
dissipates.

one less murky grey silhouette;

a glimmer of incandescence.

house of cards

Am I ready to start this next phase?

Suspended in slow motion,
I monitor the wind,
the noise,
even the humidity,
with carefully honed senses.

Inching forward,
I move the card towards its place
in the tower.

Will this next step take?
or will the whole thing come tumbling down,
again?

I want to be loved,
But I barely have enough energy to be alone.

I want to be loved.
I want to step out into that unknown.

The desire to connect is starting to bubble in my blood.
If I open that door, will everything rush at me like a flood?

I want to be loved.

The seed begins deep underground, suspending in darkness.
    "I am exactly who I need to be in this moment."

Roots start pushing their way out through the soil.
    "I am comfortable and confident in my own skin."

A shoot of green pulses upwards, breaking through the surface.
    "I deserve to feel good about myself."

The green stretches towards the sun, leaving the ground behind.
    "I am unique."

The green is strengthened, nourished from below.
    "I accept the things I cannot change."

A cluster begins to form at the top of the stalk, quivering with potential.
    "I have come this far and I can keep going."

Power surges into the cluster, feeding the frenzy.
    "I am enough."

Colour erupts into existence as each petal painstakingly unfurls.
    "I am complete."

her & i

Sometimes, I wonder where the rest of me is.
The part of me who was full of life; who was
confident she was going somewhere.

Maybe she is on a road trip.
Or in an exciting foreign place
with lots to learn.
Perhaps, she has started fresh.

I want to look for her, but I
don't know where to start.
All I can do is trust that when
it comes time for me to grow into
that part of myself again,
She will make her way back to these bones.

the music

The day was slow and cold.

I went about my business.
I thought I heard a lonesome beat,
but it disappeared when I turned off the sink.

Synth leaked out of the open doors of the fridge,
until they shut tight,
sealing the magic inside.

I opened a drawer and out poured a riff,
again to disappear as swiftly as it had begun.

Now, I thought I had been content in my silence,
but I could not let this go.

I opened the dishwasher; nothing. The dryer;
the same.

I began haphazardly yanking and shoving
each cupboard door.

The hairdryer and the blender spilled
more drums into existence.

I know I'm out of my mind, but I can't help but feel
someone is trying to tell me something.
And now that I know it exists, I can't go back to before.

My exhaustive search does not reveal
what I am so desperate the find,
and darkness falls upon the house as I slump, defeated.

It is not until I reach up and switch on the light,
that the whole house is flooded with the intricacies
and coherency of the complete song.

And finally, I can dance.

When the butterfly frees herself
from the clinging mess of her cocoon,
she will not hang around to commiserate with the
caterpillars.

Instead, she will embrace the hope of her new
existence.
She will flit from flower to flower,
float with the current of the wind,
and dance unreservedly in and out of sunbeams.

blossoming

part five

My body is a vessel of love.
I aim to fill it to the brim,
so that when it reaches full capacity,
the excess love travels over the top,
down the sides, and flows into
the hearts of the people around me.

I maintain that vessel with the idea
that it does not just belong to me,
but all the people I love.

my heart's song

Gulping water,
Solidly sleeping,
Warm sunlight.

Familiar music,
Creative projects,
Scattered birdsong.

Shared laughter,
Helpful errands,
Eccentric family.

My Heart Overflows.

My body has been a faithful friend.
She inhales the familiarity of my mother's perfume.
She savours delicious roasts.
She listens to the warbling of the magpies in the tree.
She watches lambs frolicking in the paddock.
She feels the morning sun kiss my skin.
I give her dips in the pool in the heat.
I satiate her with endless drinks of water.
I supply music to soothe her soul.
My body is a faithful friend.

Sometimes, if I lie on the grass for
long enough, out where the sun
shines and the wind whispers;
I become one with nature.

My toes wiggle off,
now stout caterpillars.

My kneecaps become crabs,
and scuttle away.

My hands transform into finches
and fly off.

The bee where my nose used to be
buzz *buzz, buzzes*.

And the positive thoughts in my head
erupt out as butterflies.

These happenings do not cause me alarm;
I am where I am meant to be.

I know when the time comes,
everyone will come rushing back,
so, I can go about my day.

I am not fully human…
I am a mountain, covered in dense foliage.
I am steady and established, ready to weather each emotion as it comes.

I am the true blue of the sky,
complimented by the rays of the sun.
I keep my slate clear and bright,
the optimal foundation for the start of a new day.

Part of me is river,
slowly bubbling and churning down its path.
I take what the day throws at me,
process it and keep it moving,
eventually letting go and watching it flow away.

I am Kookaburra,
feathers rustling in the wind.
I cackle unreservedly to appreciate every
good thing that comes into my life.
I am fully human.

I am a dusty white road,
a rusty metal cattle grid.

I am a swollen dam,
of paddocks as far as the eye can see.

I am a battered fence line in the distance,
the cool shade from the big gum trees.

I am the view from the top of the hill,
and the large rocks covered with lichen.

I am the house surrounded by gardens,
topped with a corrugated roof.

I am boisterous calves,
and frolicking lambs.

I am the earth.
I am the sky.

I am Yarra Glen.

I've seen majestic waterfalls
water flowing over
and around jutting rocks.

I've seen wide open spaces,
full of wildlife
and their antics.

I've seen rolling green country,
spotted with cows
and sheep.

I've seen the wonders of the world;
sheer cliffs
that slide down to ocean.

But the many sights I've seen
cannot compare
to the comfort
and safety
of the inside of my own house.

Dog on one side, dog on the other,
cup of tea in hand;
I am home.

I am worth a woollen jumper
and a warm pair of socks
You are worth a handful of figs
and a jar of walnuts.

You are worth a grassy hill
and a moss-covered boulder
I am worth the rain as it falls
and the snow cover on the ground.

I am worth every pebble on the beach
and every leaf on the bush
You are worth all the coral in the ocean
and all the trees on the land.

We are worth a shooting star
and the glow of the Milky Way
We are worth a golden hour
and the promise of a trip to the moon.

The sun rose, day after day.
The bees hummed in the garden,
The ants continued to march across the driveway.
And I,
I had a fire burning in my soul.
The flame was strong and bright,
and it danced,
giving off light,
even in the daytime.
It will eventually come to pass that everything becomes a story...
I hope I will remember mine with a smile.